O9-BSU-833

MAR 09 2016

301 Newark Ave
Elkton, MD 21921

Christmas
with *Southern Lady*

Christmas

with *Southern Lady*

HOLIDAY DECORATING, RECIPES & TABLE IDEAS

hm | books

hm | books

EDITORIAL

EDITORIAL DIRECTOR Andrea Fanning

CREATIVE DIRECTOR/PHOTOGRAPHY Mac Jamieson

ART DIRECTORS Leighann Lott Bryant, Ann McKeand Carothers

MANAGING EDITOR Kathleen Johnston Whaley

EDITORIAL COORDINATOR Becky Goff

ASSISTANT EDITOR Elizabeth Bonner

COPY EDITOR Nancy Ogburn

CONTRIBUTING WRITERS Karen Callaway, Annalise DeVries, Lauren Eberle

STYLISTS Amanda Bailey Leach, Tracey MacMillan Runnion, Rachael Stanton, Katherine Tucker, Adrienne Alldredge Williams

SENIOR PHOTOGRAPHERS John O'Hagan, Marcy Black Simpson

PHOTOGRAPHERS Jim Bathie, William Dickey, Stephanie Welbourne

CONTRIBUTING PHOTOGRAPHER Stephen DeVries

SENIOR DIGITAL IMAGING SPECIALIST Delisa McDaniel

DIGITAL IMAGING SPECIALIST Clark Densmore

EXECUTIVE CHEF Rebecca Treadwell Spradling

TEST KITCHEN PROFESSIONALS Allene Arnold, Kathleen Kanen, Janet Lambert, Anna Theoktisto, Loren Wood

CONTRIBUTING TEST KITCHEN PROFESSIONAL Virginia Hornbuckle

TEST KITCHEN ASSISTANT Anita Simpson Spain

DIGITAL MEDIA

MULTIMEDIA DIRECTOR Bart Clayton

ONLINE EDITOR Annalise DeVries

CONSUMER MARKETING DIRECTOR Tricia Wagner Williams

VIDEOGRAPHER Aaron Spigner

DIGITAL GRAPHIC DESIGNER Alana Hogg

ADMINISTRATIVE

HUMAN RESOURCES DIRECTOR Judy Brown Lazenby

IT DIRECTOR Matthew Scott Holt

DEALER PROGRAM MANAGER Janice Ritter

PRODUCTION ASSISTANT Rachel Collins

Front cover photography William Dickey

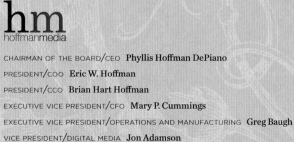

hm
hoffmanmedia

CHAIRMAN OF THE BOARD/CEO Phyllis Hoffman DePiano

PRESIDENT/COO Eric W. Hoffman

PRESIDENT/CCO Brian Hart Hoffman

EXECUTIVE VICE PRESIDENT/CFO Mary P. Cummings

EXECUTIVE VICE PRESIDENT/OPERATIONS AND MANUFACTURING Greg Baugh

VICE PRESIDENT/DIGITAL MEDIA Jon Adamson

VICE PRESIDENT/EDITORIAL Cindy Smith Cooper

VICE PRESIDENT/ADMINISTRATION Lynn Lee Terry

Copyright © 2015
by Hoffman Media

All rights reserved. No part of this book may be reproduced or transmitted in any form or by any means, electronic or mechanical, including photocopying, or by any information storage and retrieval system, without permission in writing from Hoffman Media. Reviewers may quote brief passages for specific inclusion in a magazine or newspaper.

Hoffman Media
1900 International Park Drive, Suite 50
Birmingham, Alabama 35243
www.hoffmanmedia.com

ISBN # 978-1-940772-16-5
Printed in China

Contents

Gifts *for the* Holidays

Goodies to Give 12
All Wrapped Up 18

Decor *for the* Holidays

White Christmas 28
Southern Style 36
Rustic Charm 42
Christmas on the Mountain 48
Southern Splendor 56
Wreaths for the Holidays 62

Settings *for the* Holidays

The Holly and the Ivy 72
O Christmas Tree 80
The First Noel 86
I Saw Three Ships 92
Joy to the World 98

Fare *for the* Holidays

Enticing Appetizers 104
Seasonal Sippers 112
Delectable Sides 120
Decadent Deserts 128
Family Gathering 136

INTRODUCTION 9
ACKNOWLEDGMENTS 158

Christmas MAY COME BUT ONCE A YEAR

on the calendar, but for our staff, it is a yearlong event—and we wouldn't have it any other way.

From decorating trees to dreaming up desserts, our team gets positively giddy over producing

seasonal themes and creative ideas to make the season bright. This compilation includes a variety

of wreaths, garlands, and other home-decorating flourishes to honor this festive time of year,

and in our Settings chapter, you'll find a special series of tablescapes. With even a few notes of

"The First Noel" or "Joy to the World," the Christmas spirit rises and shines, and through the art

of hospitality, we turned some of our favorite, time-honored tunes into a holiday showcase with

plenty of panache. You'll also find a thoughtful selection of go-to recipes for party hopping and

at-home hostessing, and in true *Southern Lady* style, each page is designed to help you extend

season's greetings from the porch to the parlor and beyond. We sincerely hope the sweet refrains

of the memories you make this Christmas echo with joy for years to come.

for the Gifts HOLIDAYS

Spread the spirit of Christmas with homemade gifts from your kitchen and creatively wrapped presents under the tree.

Goodies TO GIVE

These tasty treats in pretty packages deliver the sweetest holiday surprises.

WHITE CHOCOLATE SNACK MIX
Makes 15 to 20 servings

6 cups honey graham cereal
6 cups crispy corn cereal squares
6 cups frosted toasted oat cereal
4 cups roasted salted pistachios
4 cups salted sunflower kernels
½ (1-pound) bag mini pretzel twists
3 (5-ounce) bags dried cranberries
4 (11-ounce) bags white chocolate
    morsels, melted

1. In a large roasting pan, combine cereals, pistachios, sunflower kernels, pretzels, and cranberries. Drizzle melted white chocolate over cereal mixture, stirring gently to coat. Store in an airtight container.

Quick-AND-EASY *recipes* WILL DELIGHT EVERYONE ON YOUR *Christmas* LIST.

OPPOSITES ATTRACT
This blend of sweet-and-salty tidbits makes an irresistible flavor combination. Be sure to mix up plenty—it disappears by the handful.

WHITE CHOCOLATE POPCORN
Makes 12 servings

24 cups popped popcorn
4 cups whole almonds
1 cup butter
2 cups firmly packed light brown sugar
½ cup light corn syrup
Coarse kosher salt to taste
2 (11-ounce) bags white chocolate
   morsels, melted

1. Preheat oven to 250°. Place popcorn and almonds in a large roasting pan; set aside.
2. In a medium saucepan, heat butter over medium heat until melted. Add brown sugar and corn syrup, stirring until sugar is dissolved. Bring mixture to a boil, stirring occasionally. Cook for 5 minutes, or until mixture registers 270° on a candy thermometer. Working quickly, pour sugar mixture over popcorn, stirring until popcorn and almonds are evenly coated. Sprinkle with kosher salt, stirring to combine well. Bake for 1 hour, stirring every 15 minutes. Remove from oven, and drizzle melted white chocolate over popcorn in pan, stirring until popcorn and pecans are evenly coated. Immediately spread popcorn onto parchment paper to cool. Store in an airtight container.

NUTTY BUT NICE
Buttery popcorn and crunchy almonds melted together with sweet white chocolate morsels—need we say more? You will love every tasty bite.

SALTED CARAMEL TURTLES
Makes about 4 dozen

8 cups pecan halves
2 (12-ounce) bags semisweet chocolate
   morsels, melted
3 cups sugar
2 cups heavy whipping cream
1½ cups light corn syrup
Coarse kosher salt

1. In a large bowl, combine pecan halves and melted chocolate, stirring to coat. Drop pecan mixture by rounded tablespoonfuls 2 inches apart onto parchment paper. Let stand for 1 hour, or until chocolate is set.

2. In a large heavy-bottomed Dutch oven, combine sugar, cream, and corn syrup over medium-high heat. Stir constantly until sugar mixture registers 240° on a candy thermometer. Remove from heat, and let cool until sugar mixture registers 190°. Spoon mixture over top of each pecan cluster, and sprinkle with kosher salt. Let stand for 1 hour, or until completely cool. Store in an airtight container.

CHOCOLATE CHIP ESPRESSO COOKIES
Makes about 18 cookies

1 cup butter, softened
1 cup sugar
1 cup firmly packed light brown sugar
2 large eggs
2 teaspoons vanilla extract
2 cups all-purpose flour
1 cup whole-wheat flour
1 teaspoon baking soda
1 teaspoon salt
¼ cup hot water
1 tablespoon espresso powder
1 (11.5-ounce) bag semisweet chocolate chunks

1. Preheat oven to 350°. Line 2 baking sheets with parchment paper.
2. In a large bowl, beat butter at medium-high speed with a mixer for 2 minutes or until creamy. Add sugar and brown sugar, and beat for 2 minutes or until fluffy. Add eggs, one at a time, beating well after each addition. Add vanilla, beating well.
3. In a large bowl, sift together all-purpose flour, whole-wheat flour, baking soda, and salt. Gradually add flour mixture to butter mixture, beating well after each addition.
4. In a small measuring cup, combine hot water and espresso, stirring to dissolve. Add 3 tablespoons espresso to butter mixture, beating well. Add chocolate chunks, beating to combine. Scoop dough by ¼ cupfuls, and drop at least 3 inches apart onto prepared baking sheets. Bake for 10 to 12 minutes, or until lightly golden. Let cool on pan for 2 minutes. Let cool completely on a wire rack.

merry merry

WHITE CHOCOLATE APRICOT BARS
Makes 2 dozen bars

1½ cups all-purpose flour
¾ cup firmly packed light brown sugar
½ cup plus 2 tablespoons cold butter, divided
2 cups finely chopped cashews, divided
1 cup white chocolate morsels
½ cup light corn syrup
1 tablespoon water
1 cup chopped dried apricots
Garnish: melted white chocolate

1. Preheat oven to 350°. In a medium bowl, combine flour and brown sugar. Using a pastry blender, cut in ½ cup butter until mixture resembles coarse crumbs. Stir in ½ cup cashews. Press mixture evenly into bottom of a 13x9-inch baking pan; bake for 10 minutes.
2. In a small saucepan over medium heat, combine white chocolate morsels, corn syrup, remaining 2 tablespoons butter, and water. Bring to a boil; cook for 2 minutes, stirring constantly. Pour white chocolate mixture over crust. Sprinkle with remaining 1½ cups cashews and apricots. Bake for 16 to 18 minutes, or until lightly browned. Drizzle with melted white chocolate, if desired.

DOUBLY DELICIOUS
Enjoy twice the goodness with these fruity bars. Not only are they packed with morsels of white chocolate, they are drizzled with it, too!

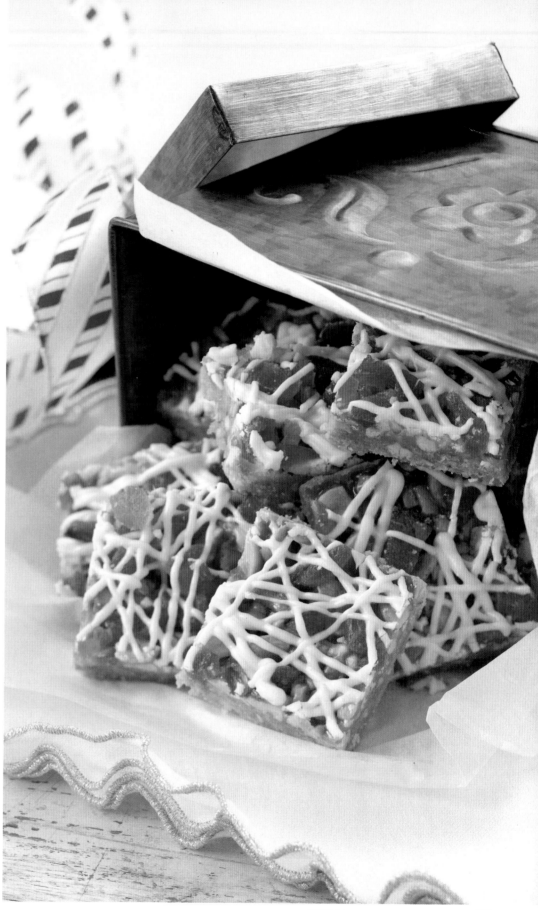

FOR YOU.

Lucy

to John

All *Wrapped* UP

Crafted with love and care, beautiful packages become part of the merry decor.

COTTAGE APPEAL

Vintage prints, chunky yarn, and lace accents lend beaucoups of charm to a cottage Christmas. Even brown craft paper takes on an elegant look when wrapped with twine and sprigs of greenery.

Merry Christmas

ARTISTIC INTERPRETATIONS

Peruse your own home for everyday inspiration. Get creative with spools of leftover ribbon and yarn to arrange an eclectic compilation of pretty ties under the tree. Sticky scrapbook letters, available at crafts stores, add a fun flourish. Pay homage to the holiday's natural splendor, and adorn packages with sparkling snowflakes and pinecones.

FAUX SNOW

Arrange a winter wonderland beneath your tree by adding doilies and lace to your cache of frills. Whether layered on a package or used to gussy up a basic gift bag, the dainty and budget-friendly adornments will make each gift unique—just like snowflakes.

GRAPHIC TAGS

Rather than hide away tags beneath the gift, make them the focal point of the presentation. Bold graphics from extra greeting cards work perfectly, as do repurposed holiday photo cards; recipients will cherish the nod to Christmases past. Use oversize monograms as the focal point of a package to add a personal touch and classic sophistication.

happy holidays

MIX & MATCH
Pair eye-catching patterns with solid colors to create contrast among the wrapped surprises under the tree. Metallic elements enhance the holly jolly collection.

Peace, love, happiness

PEACE & JOY

Season's Greetings

PEACE LOVE JOY

Decor for the HOLIDAYS

Step inside these beautifully appointed homes that reflect the warmth, excitement, and pure jubilance that is the signature of Christmas.

White
CHRISTMAS

*Invite the spirit of the season into your home
with natural tones of white, cream, and green,
creating an elegant holiday retreat
for family and friends.*

BRINGING NATURE IN

Fresh greenery paints a rich, crisp image among the white canvas of the walls. A stunning swag of tree trimmings and celadon-colored silk ribbon highlight an already captivating staircase, while boxwood wreaths and live accents fill spaces in the entryway and beyond.

A TOUCH OF *sparkle*
AND RICH *gold* BESTOWS
A GRACEFUL *glow*
ON THE DASHING
ambiance.

SIMPLY BEAUTIFUL

Sparse white lights shine against a freshly cut tree. A palette still in keeping with your tones can be achieved even when mixing sentimental handmade ornaments from little hands and delicate, treasured collectibles. A touch of Southern flair is found in the striking magnolia-leaf wreath that pulls attention to the fireplace mantel. Assorted sizes of white candles, a pair of lofty ornamental candleholders, and a garland intertwined with fresh trimmings and strands of metallic beads complete the grand display.

WINTER WONDERMENT

Create an awe-inspiring floral centerpiece for the dining room table with the continued hues of white and green. In this arrangement, white amaryllis provides graceful height. Found in the living room, an already beautifully detailed candle sconce gets a holiday update with trimmings and a celadon ribbon. The use of verdant wreaths, though simple in design, can make quite a magical impact throughout the home.

Southern STYLE

A classic Southern colonial home shines with traditional touches for the holiday season.

YULETIDE DINING

A cozy dining room, warmed by a welcoming fire, is the ideal place to host a Christmas meal for the family. The windows are adorned with feathery cedar boughs, accented with cranberry-hued ribbon.

FINER THINGS

This centerpiece captures the beauty of the holidays with colorful fruit and flowers. Dinnerware continues the floral motif, and flickering candles reveal all of the delightful details. Gold accents dance across the room and bring a regal touch to the tablescape.

Rustic CHARM

*A rustic home is decked out for the holidays,
using natural elements that sync with its everyday style.*

EASY ELEGANCE

A quieter palette can be just as festive as its brighter cousins. Choose a traditional Christmas china pattern to anchor the scene, then fashion a casual centerpiece with citrus, apples, and greenery.

'ROUND THE TREE

Plan a fun-filled decor theme around a cheery Christmas tree. Retro-inspired large, colorful bulbs cast a joyful glow, and clusters of cut magnolia leaves tucked here and there give the display a Southern accent.

SYLVAN SPLENDOR

From the porch to the parlor to the kitchen, add a dose of merriment with freshly clipped greenery. Further the look and feel of a country Christmas with thoughtful details. After guests have traveled over the river and through the woods, the sight of holiday accents paired with cute-as-can-be woodland critters is sure to illicit plenty of gleeful grins.

Christmas
on the
MOUNTAIN

*A rustic retreat offers the ideal setting
for a cozy holiday gathering.*

PURE SIMPLICITY

This home's rural surroundings call for homespun decorations, like the entry's simple boxwood wreath and a centerpiece of loosely composed boughs.

SOUTHERN SLANT

Take the party to the porch where a whitewashed table is set with wood slices that serve as chargers. The candles in the chandelier's votives are held in place with fresh cranberries, and greenery is threaded through the frame. Flatware is tied with ribbon and sprigs of white pine.

NATURAL NOEL

Throughout the home, accents from nature lend subtle yet festive touches. A garland of pine, magnolia, and holly adorns the mantel, while a similar composition stands in a wooden vase on the coffee table. Bright red poinsettias and berries are artfully placed in the space, and narcissus blooms line the dining table.

SEASONAL SLUMBER

Red toile bedding brings Christmas charm to the master bedroom. In keeping with the theme, a wreath of mixed greenery is hung with linen ribbon from the timber bed frame, and swags combining fir and pine branches are tied at the footboard.

268

Southern
SPLENDOR

*Christmas is knocking on your door, bringing with it a
season of warmth and celebration for all who enter.*

These homeowners turned both the front and back porches into jolly retreats. With sentimental treasures in classic red and green, the vignettes inspire memories of Decembers past, and the exteriors, dressed in holiday style, light up the neighborhood with the feeling of Christmas.

SIGNS OF THE SEASON

From porches to screened-in patios, outdoor areas provide a ready canvas for the whimsical side of holiday decorating. Rethink traditional tree-trimming elements like skirts and glass spires, and opt for more weather-hardy ones, such as a galvanized tub for the base and a fanciful wired embellishment for the top. Nostalgic details and kid-friendly touches are right at home in the mirthful mix. Take advantage of the mild Southern weather, and set a casual table for smaller family meals.

fresh ELEMENTS AND ELEGANT *details* COMBINE FOR A *lovely* WINTER SETTING.

Wreaths for the HOLIDAYS

Make a beautiful first impression with these welcoming symbols of the season.

GRAND GREETING

Let the celebration start at the front door by framing it with an evergreen garland. Then accent a sumptuous wreath of mixed greenery with pinecones and a bow of richly textured ribbon in Christmas hues.

FRESH & FLORAL

Whether you want to try your hand at a DIY version or collaborate with your local florist, a one-of-a-kind wreath not only complements your home décor, it also adds scores of personality. Take a delightful departure from traditional components, and fashion a wreath made from citrus fruits to hang in the kitchen or breakfast nook. Simply wire an assortment of lemons, kumquats, and clementines to a standard form, and fill in with sprigs of lime-green foliage. If you prefer more conventional colors, the glossy green of magnolia leaves pairs beautifully with velvety red Freedom roses, hypericum berries, Pink Lady apples, and cherries. This style wreath offers lots of visual impact and is a timeless way to dress up your front door. For a fabulous floral display sure to garner rave reviews, form a foundation of lacy cedar sprigs, and embellish with coral cymbidium orchids and scarlet roses. Hypericum berries, dried seed pods, and other pretties serve as festive fillers.

USE A BIT OF
imagination
TO *create* A
DELIGHTFUL CIRCLE OF
Christmas
CHEER.

ELFIN MAGIC

Channel your inner child for a whimsical wreath made from camellia foliage, fresh greenery, red and green carnations, and of course, a few of Santa's favorite friends. Add a strand of old-fashioned lights for even more fun.

VINTAGE FINDS

Spools from an old mill in Scotland inspired this vintage-look adornment. Ivory spray roses, cotton, and brunia berries are radiant against a backdrop of varied foliage, while buttons and bottlebrush ornaments further the ensemble's nostalgic tone.

NATURAL ATTRACTION

The makings for spectacular wreaths are all around us, and these eye-catching examples illustrate that point perfectly. For an elegant, glitzy greeting, attach magnolia wreaths that have been covered in white lacquer spray paint to a standard wreath form. Add a shimmery dusting of European glass glitter to a circlet of hypericum berries, and place in the center. Say welcome in true Southern style by flipping magnolia leaves to show the bronze underside and alternating with dried okra pods. Or incorporate a few sentimental treasures—like the brass-charm wreath and bells, shown here—in a laurel made of feathery cedar boughs, dried sedum, and pinecones.

Settings *for the* HOLIDAYS

Gather around the holiday table with those you hold dear to celebrate blessings abundant at this special time of year.

The Holly and the IVY

Usher Christmas in with rich colors and fresh floral creations that lend a regal ambiance to your holiday meal.

THE *holly-and-ivy* THEME THREADS *beautifully* THROUGHOUT THIS *charming* *Christmas* TABLEAU.

GOLDEN TOUCH

Brilliant gold chargers set off the intricate design of the lovely holiday dinnerware, and the vibrant reds and greens in the arrangements of holly and roses further the room's elegant atmosphere. Gilded accents shine here, there, and everywhere—encircling the stemware, framing the place card, and shimmering in both the silken napkins and napkin rings. A coordinating tea set brings added brilliance to this classic Christmas setting.

SIMPLY SPLENDID

Create an eye-catching display by weaving cedar trimmings with holly and ivy into the chandelier. It makes a stunning design set among the hanging crystal prisms. On the buffet, ornate tussie mussies hold cheerful bouquets, and when grouped with more greenery and berries, they lend a decidedly Southern and elegant holiday feel to the dining room. To complete the scene, an exquisite Nativity takes center stage atop gold-trimmed linens and serves as a lovely reminder of the reason for the season.

O. Christmas TREE

Nothing is lovelier than a setting inspired by the wondrous beauty that a Christmas tree brings to the season.

DELIGHTFUL DETAILS

Often the focal point of holiday decorating, the Chritmas tree emits glee and inspires seasonal flourishes throughout the home. Coordinate charming fir tree–inspired china with a larger dish in a harmonizing hue. Place upon a subtly detailed gold charger. Keep the setting simple with white lace napkins. A magnolia-leaf garland entwined with red mesh ribbon becomes an attractive fireplace accent, and with the addition of oversize ornaments and a pretty and petite magnolia-leaf wreath, the mantel decor is complete.

"CHRISTMAS WAVES A *magic* WAND OVER THIS WORLD, AND BEHOLD, *everything* IS *softer* AND MORE *beautiful*."

—Norman Vincent Peale

The First NOEL

Bring a dash of panache to the holidays by fashioning a French-influenced setting filled with style.

paula

Pretty in pink, the accents for this enchanting setting rely on ivory and taupe to form the foundation and keep the scene elegant. Feminine flourishes pirouette around the Christmas tree and joyfully echo in the the rose-filled centerpiece.

OOH LA LOVELY!

Celebrate Joyeux Noël with an enchanting holiday setting that would be equally at home in a Parisian parlor. Tiny Limoges boxes are perfect for holding place cards etched in gilded script, and they are also a pretty way to incorporate cherished collectibles into the scene. Think pink with exquisite raspberry-trimmed china by Herend, and add an extravagant bouquet of roses nestled in a lovely bas-relief vase. For shimmer and shine, bring in lighted trees, iridescent gift wrap and ribbons, and flickering pillar candles.

FRENCH-*inspired* ACCENTS LEND A *Continental* CHARM TO THIS *sophisticated* SETTING.

I Saw
Three
SHIPS

*Honor the Christmas Day sighting of three
sailing ships with an ethereal palette and
whimsical, homespun details.*

Use layers and levels to make ordinary objects feel extraordinary. Handmade ships inspire the vibe, and an artful composition of household treasures—silver platters, weathered wood, vintage books, and antique ornaments—brings whimsy and depth to the armada of decor.

PERFECT PAIRING

The Old-World style of this tableau presents a perfect excuse to display handmade trinkets with heirloom treasures. Stamped greetings on a group of old novels lend an air of cottage charm, while mercury glass ups the glamour. Vintage holiday finds and handsome antiques increase the appeal and complement the nontraditional tree.

Joy to the WORLD

Return to a simpler time, and create a merry air about your child's playroom in rustic and retro Christmas fashion.

OH, WHAT FUN!

Turn the children's table into the place to be. Tartan fabric and tree stumps set a casual tone. With a set of crayons, wee ones can draw their own place mat on the craft-paper table topper. A hanging lantern lends extra light to this playful space, and a plush wall mount is oh, so "deer."

Happy DETAILS BRING HOLIDAY *cheer* TO THIS SPECIAL *setting* DESIGNED TO GIVE *children* A PLACE OF THEIR OWN.

Fare for the
HOLIDAYS

Sip and savor the flavors of the season with these incredibly delicious dishes that salute the joys of Yuletide gatherings.

Enticing APPETIZERS

*Set out any of these flavorful hors d'oeuvres
for an elegant start to a memorable gathering.*

CHEDDAR OLIVE PUFFS
Makes about 4 dozen

3 cups all-purpose baking mix*
1 teaspoon garlic powder
¼ teaspoon ground red pepper
4 cups shredded Cheddar cheese
2 cups chopped green olives with
    pimientos
3 large eggs, lightly beaten

1. Preheat oven to 350°. Spray 3 rimmed baking sheets with nonstick cooking spray.
2. In a large bowl, combine baking mix, garlic powder, and red pepper. Add cheese and olives, stirring to combine well. Add eggs, stirring until dry ingredients are moistened. Shape mixture into 1½-inch balls, and place, 1 inch apart, on prepared baking sheets. Bake for 20 to 25 minutes, or until lightly browned.

For testing purposes, we used Bisquick.

CHEESY ITALIAN SAUSAGE DIP
Makes 10 to 12 servings

2 tablespoons olive oil
1 (19-ounce) package hot Italian
    sausage, casings removed
1 large red bell pepper, diced
1 large yellow bell pepper, diced
1 large green bell pepper, diced
1 large yellow onion, chopped
2 (8-ounce) blocks Monterey Jack
    cheese, shredded
1 (8-ounce) block mozzarella cheese,
    shredded
1 (16-ounce) container sour cream

1. Preheat oven to 350°.
2. In a large skillet, heat olive oil
over medium heat. Add sausage,
bell peppers, and onion. Cook for 15
minutes, stirring frequently, until
sausage is browned. Drain well.
3. In a large bowl, combine sausage
mixture, cheeses, and sour cream,
stirring to combine well. Spoon mixture
into a 2-quart baking dish. Bake for 20 to
25 minutes, or until bubbly.

*TIP: Keep this hearty dip warm in a
chafing dish or slow cooker.*

CHICKEN AND BROCCOLI PHYLLO SQUARES
Makes about 2 dozen

1 cup ricotta cheese
4 large eggs, lightly beaten
¾ teaspoon salt
¼ teaspoon ground black pepper
1 bunch green onions, finely chopped
2 tablespoons chopped fresh thyme
4 cups chopped cooked chicken
3 cups finely chopped cooked broccoli
3 cups finely shredded Parmesan cheese
1 (8-ounce) block feta cheese, crumbled
½ (1-pound) box phyllo sheets, thawed
1 cup butter, melted

1. Preheat oven to 350°.
2. In a large bowl, combine ricotta cheese, eggs, salt, and pepper. Add green onions and thyme, stirring to combine. Add chicken, broccoli, Parmesan cheese, and feta cheese, stirring to combine well. Fit 1 phyllo sheet in the bottom of a lightly greased 13x9-inch baking pan. Brush well with melted butter. Fit 7 more phyllo sheets in pan, one at a time, brushing each layer well with melted butter.
3. Spread one-third of chicken mixture over phyllo. Add 3 more phyllo sheets, brushing each with melted butter, then another one-third of chicken mixture; repeat layers. Top chicken mixture with 8 phyllo sheets, brushing each layer well with melted butter. Using a sharp knife, score the top layers of phyllo into squares before baking. Bake for 40 minutes.

CHEESE PUFFS WITH TOASTED PECAN AND BACON FILLING
Makes about 2½ dozen

1 cup water
½ cup butter
1 cup all-purpose flour
½ teaspoon salt
4 large eggs
1 cup finely grated Gruyère cheese
2 (8-ounce) packages cream cheese, softened
¼ cup sour cream
1 pound hickory-smoked bacon, cooked and crumbled
1 cup chopped toasted pecans
¼ cup chopped fresh parsley
2 tablespoons chopped fresh chives
¼ teaspoon ground black pepper

1. Preheat oven to 400°. Line baking sheets with parchment paper.
2. In a small saucepan, bring water and butter to a boil over medium heat. Using a wooden spoon, beat in flour and salt, stirring constantly, until mixture forms a ball. Remove pan from heat, and let cool for 5 minutes. Add eggs, one at a time, beating with wooden spoon for 30 seconds after each addition until smooth. Add Gruyère cheese, stirring until smooth. Using a piping bag fitted with a star tip, pipe 1½-inch mounds, 2 inches apart, onto prepared baking sheets.
3. Bake for 20 minutes, or until golden and puffy; let cool on wire rack. Cut out top of each pastry; pull out and discard soft dough inside.
4. In a medium bowl, combine cream cheese and sour cream. Beat at medium speed with a mixer until smooth. Add bacon, pecans, parsley, chives, and pepper, beating to combine. Spoon cream cheese mixture into bottoms of cheese puffs. Cover with tops.

DILL SHRIMP DIP
Makes 10 to 12 servings

2 (8-ounce) packages cream cheese,
  softened
1 (16-ounce) container sour cream
½ cup mayonnaise
¼ cup chopped fresh dill
1 teaspoon lemon zest
2 tablespoons fresh lemon juice
3 tablespoons minced green onion
2 tablespoons capers, rinsed and chopped
2 teaspoons Worcestershire sauce
1 teaspoon seasoned salt
2 pounds chopped cooked shrimp
Garnish: cooked shrimp, fresh dill

1. In a large bowl, combine cream cheese, sour cream, mayonnaise, dill, lemon zest, lemon juice, green onion, capers, Worcestershire sauce, and seasoned salt. Beat at medium speed with a mixer until well combined. Stir in shrimp. Garnish with cooked shrimp and dill, if desired. Serve with crackers.

SPINACH AND PARMESAN MUSHROOMS
Makes 2 dozen

24 baby portobello or cremini
   mushrooms
¼ cup butter, melted
½ cup butter
1 tablespoon minced garlic
1 bunch green onions, chopped
2 (10-ounce) packages frozen chopped
   spinach, thawed and squeezed dry
1 tablespoon fresh lemon juice
1 teaspoon salt
½ teaspoon pepper
2 cups finely grated Parmesan cheese
½ cup panko (Japanese bread crumbs)
2 tablespoons chopped fresh parsley
Garnish: toasted panko

1. Preheat oven to 350°.
2. Remove stems from mushrooms. Wipe caps clean, using a damp paper towel. Brush mushrooms with ¼ cup melted butter, and place on a rimmed baking sheet; set aside. In a large skillet, heat ½ cup butter over medium heat until melted. Add garlic; cook for 1 minute, stirring constantly. Add green onion, spinach, lemon juice, salt, and pepper; cook for 4 to 5 minutes, stirring frequently. Remove from heat, and let cool for 10 minutes. Stir in Parmesan cheese, panko, and parsley. Spoon spinach mixture into mushrooms. Bake for 20 to 25 minutes. Garnish with toasted panko, if desired.

ROAST BEEF SLIDERS WITH GREEN ONION REMOULADE
Makes 2½ dozen

2 cups warm milk (105° to 110°)
2 (0.25-ounce) packages active dry yeast
½ cup sugar, divided
7 to 8 cups bread flour
1 tablespoon salt
1 cup vegetable oil
2 large eggs, lightly beaten
¼ cup butter, melted and divided
2 pounds thinly sliced deli roast beef
Green Onion Remoulade (recipe follows)

1. In a small bowl, combine warm milk, yeast, and ¼ cup sugar; let stand for 5 minutes. In a medium bowl, combine 7 cups bread flour, remaining ¼ cup sugar, and salt.
2. In the bowl of a stand mixer fitted with a dough hook, combine milk mixture, oil, and eggs. Gradually add flour mixture to milk mixture, beating until smooth after each addition. Beat in enough remaining flour to make a soft dough.
3. Turn dough out onto a lightly floured surface; knead until smooth and elastic, about 5 minutes. Place dough in a lightly greased bowl, turning to grease top. Cover, and let stand in a warm place (85°), free from drafts, for 1 to 1½ hours or until doubled in size.
4. Punch dough down; cover, and let stand for 10 minutes.
5. Brush a 13x9-inch baking pan with 2 tablespoons melted butter. Divide dough into 30 equal pieces (about 2 inches in diameter); shape each piece into a ball. Place balls, side by side, in prepared pan. Brush tops of dough with remaining 2 tablespoons melted butter. Cover, and let rise in a warm place (85°), free from drafts, for 1 hour or until doubled in size.
6. Preheat oven to 350°. Bake for 15 to 20 minutes or until lightly browned. Let cool completely in pan.
7. To serve, split each roll in half horizontally. Spread Green Onion Remoulade on bottom halves of rolls. Layer roast beef on bottom halves of prepared rolls. Top with additional remoulade and tops of rolls. Serve immediately.

Green Onion Remoulade
Makes about 1½ cups

1 cup mayonnaise
1 bunch green onions, green part only
¼ cup sweet pickle relish
¼ cup dill pickle relish
2 tablespoons chopped fresh parsley
2 tablespoons Creole mustard
¼ teaspoon ground black pepper

1. In the work bowl of a food processor, combine mayonnaise, green onions, sweet pickle relish, dill pickle relish, parsley, Creole mustard, and pepper. Process until well blended. Cover, and refrigerate for at least 1 hour.

Seasonal SIPPERS

Both spirited and soul warming, this collection of beverages positively spills over with holiday cheer.

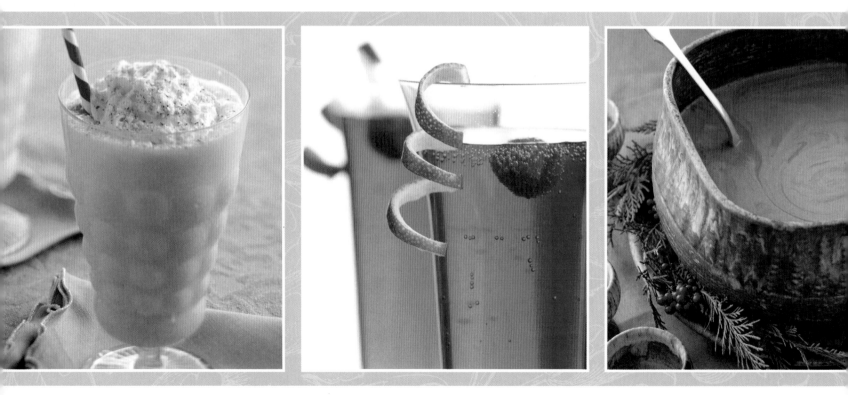

CRANBERRY PEAR ROSEMARY CIDER

Makes about 3 quarts

1 (64-ounce) bottle cranberry juice
1 (33.8-ounce) bottle pear nectar
1 tablespoon whole cloves
1 large sprig rosemary
Garnish: fresh rosemary, fresh cranberries

1. In a large Dutch oven, combine cranberry juice, pear nectar, cloves, and rosemary. Bring to a simmer over medium heat for 20 minutes. Remove cloves and rosemary. Garnish with fresh rosemary and fresh cranberries, if desired.

GINGERBREAD LATTE
Makes 4 servings

2½ cups half-and-half
1 teaspoon vanilla extract
½ cup freshly brewed strong espresso
½ cup molasses
2 teaspoons ground ginger

1. In a medium saucepan, combine half-and-half and vanilla over medium heat. Whisking constantly, heat for 5 minutes, or until milk begins to steam; do not boil. Remove from heat. Add espresso, molasses, and ginger, whisking to combine.

LOVE A LATTE
No need for an espresso machine at home; simply whisking will create that signature foam on top. If desired, add sugar for a sweeter latte.

SPARKLING CHRISTMAS COCKTAIL
Makes 8 to 10 servings

1 (750-milliliter) bottle
   Prosecco, chilled
2 cups cranberry-raspberry
   juice, chilled
2 tablespoons fresh lime juice
2 tablespoons grenadine
1 tablespoon raspberry liqueur
1 tablespoon orange liqueur
Garnish: fresh raspberries,
   lime curls

1. In a pitcher, combine Prosecco, cranberry-raspberry juice, lime juice, grenadine, raspberry liqueur, and orange liqueur, stirring gently to combine. Serve chilled. Garnish with fresh raspberries and lime curls, if desired.

HOLIDAY ICED TEA
Makes about 2½ quarts

3 quarts water
3 cinnamon sticks
1 tablespoon whole allspice
1 tablespoon whole cardamom pods
1 lemon, sliced
4 family-size tea bags
1½ cups sugar
2 tablespoons fresh lemon juice
Garnish: cinnamon sticks, lemon slices

1. In a large saucepan, combine water, cinnamon sticks, allspice, cardamom, and lemon. Bring to a boil over medium-high heat. Reduce heat to medium, and cook for 10 minutes. Remove from heat, and add tea bags. Cover, and steep for 5 minutes. Strain tea into a large pitcher. Add sugar and lemon juice, stirring until sugar dissolves. Serve over ice. Garnish with cinnamon sticks and lemon slices, if desired.

CHOCOLATE MILK PUNCH
Makes about 1 gallon

½ gallon whole milk
1½ cups Irish cream liqueur
¾ cup bourbon
½ cup chocolate liqueur
½ teaspoon vanilla extract
1 quart chocolate ice cream, softened

1. In a large pitcher, combine milk, Irish cream liqueur, bourbon, chocolate liqueur, and vanilla. Add ice cream, stirring to combine. Cover and chill.

PEPPERMINT MILK SHAKES
Makes 4 servings

4 cups vanilla ice cream
1½ cups whole milk
½ cup finely crushed peppermint
Garnish: whipped cream, crushed peppermint

1. In the container of a blender, combine ice cream, milk, and peppermint. Process until well combined. Garnish with whipped cream and crushed peppermint, if desired.

DRESSED TO IMPRESS

Make special-occasion drinks all the more festive with finishing touches, such as a garnish, a pretty stirring stick, or an old-fashioned straw.

POMEGRANATE GINGER MARTINI
Makes 1 drink

4 ounces pomegranate juice
1 ounce gin*
½ ounce Ginger Simple Syrup
  (recipe follows)

1. Fill a cocktail shaker halfway with ice cubes. Add pomegranate juice, gin, and Ginger Simple Syrup. Shake mixture vigorously for 5 to 10 seconds. Strain mixture into glass.

For testing purposes, we used Bombay Sapphire Gin.

Ginger Simple Syrup
Makes about 1 cup

1 cup sugar
1 cup water
1 (2-inch) piece fresh gingerroot,
  cut into pieces

1. In a small saucepan, combine sugar, water, and gingerroot over medium-high heat; stir until sugar dissolves. Cook for 5 minutes. Remove from heat. Cover, and steep for 30 minutes. Strain syrup, and let cool completely. Store in an airtight container for up to 2 weeks.

Delectable SIDES

Delight guests with a savory selection of sides, from colorful casseroles to new takes on old favorites.

CREAMY CORN

Makes 10 to 12 servings

8 slices hickory-smoked bacon
6 cups fresh corn kernels
   (about 8 to 10 ears)
1 large yellow onion, chopped
1 tablespoon minced garlic
¼ cup all-purpose flour
2 cups heavy whipping cream
1 teaspoon sugar
1 teaspoon salt
¼ teaspoon ground red pepper

1. In a large skillet, cook bacon over medium heat for 6 to 7 minutes, until crisp. Remove from pan, and crumble, reserving drippings in pan. To skillet, add corn, onion, and garlic; cook for 15 minutes, stirring frequently, until tender. Add flour; cook for 2 minutes, stirring constantly. Gradually add cream, stirring to combine. Stir in sugar, salt, and red pepper. Cook for 2 minutes, until heated through. Top with crumbled bacon.

WILD RICE CASSEROLE
Makes 10 to 12 servings

3 cups chicken broth
2 cups wild rice blend*
1 (19-ounce) package hot Italian
  sausage, casings removed
2 tablespoons olive oil
2 (8-ounce) containers sliced baby
  portobello mushrooms
1 large yellow onion, chopped
1 tablespoon minced garlic
1 (10.5-ounce) can cream of
  mushroom soup
1 (8-ounce) container sour cream
½ teaspoon salt
Garnish: chopped tomato,
  chopped fresh parsley

1. Preheat oven to 350°. In a large saucepan, combine chicken broth and rice over medium-high heat. Bring to a boil. Reduce heat to low, and cook, covered, for 15 minutes. Remove from heat, and let stand, covered, for 10 minutes. Fluff rice with a fork.

2. In a large skillet, cook sausage over medium heat for 12 to 15 minutes, or until browned; drain and set aside. In skillet, heat olive oil over medium heat. Add mushrooms, onion, and garlic; cook for 15 minutes, stirring frequently, until tender. In a large bowl, combine rice, sausage, mushroom mixture, mushroom soup, sour cream, and salt, stirring to combine well. Spoon rice mixture into a 13x9-inch baking dish. Bake for 30 minutes. Garnish with chopped tomato and parsley, if desired.

For testing purposes, we used RiceSelect Royal Blend.

ROASTED GARLIC
MASHED POTATOES
Makes 8 to 10 servings

3 quarts water
2 pounds Yukon Gold potatoes, diced
2 pounds red potatoes, diced
1 tablespoon plus 1¼ teaspoons salt,
   divided
½ cup butter, softened
1 (8-ounce) package cream cheese,
   softened
3 heads garlic, roasted (see below)
½ cup sour cream
½ teaspoon ground black pepper
Garnish: chopped fresh chives

1. In a large Dutch oven, combine water, Yukon Gold potatoes, red potatoes, and 1 tablespoon salt. Bring to a boil; cook for 10 to 15 minutes, or until tender. Drain potatoes well, and return to saucepan. Add butter and cream cheese; using a potato masher, mash potato mixture until butter is melted. Add roasted garlic, sour cream, remaining 1¼ teaspoons salt, and pepper, stirring to combine well. Garnish with chives, if desired.

ROASTING GARLIC

To roast garlic, cut tops off heads, and drizzle heads with olive oil; wrap in foil, and bake at 400° for 1 hour. Let garlic cool, then squeeze cloves out of their skins.

BAKED EGGPLANT PARMESAN
Makes 10 to 12 servings

Olive oil for frying
4 large eggplants (peeled and sliced
   into ½-inch rounds)
1 teaspoon garlic powder
½ teaspoon salt
¼ teaspoon ground black pepper
3 cups shredded mozzarella cheese
1½ cups finely grated Parmigiano-
   Reggiano cheese
1 large red bell pepper, chopped
1 bunch green onion, chopped
2 cups Italian seasoned panko
   (Japanese bread crumbs)
¼ cup butter, melted

1. Preheat oven to 350°. In a large nonstick skillet, heat 2 tablespoons olive oil over medium-high heat. Working in batches, cook eggplant slices for 2 to 3 minutes per side, until lightly browned, adding oil as needed. In a 13x9-inch baking dish, layer one-third of eggplant.
2. In a small bowl, combine garlic powder, salt, and pepper. Sprinkle eggplant with one-third garlic-powder mixture. Top with one-third mozzarella cheese, one-third Parmigiano-Reggiano cheese, one-third bell pepper, and one-third green onion. Add 2 more layers of remaining eggplant, garlic-powder mixture, cheese, and vegetables.
3. In a small bowl, combine panko and melted butter, tossing to coat. Sprinkle on top of eggplant. Bake for 10 to 15 minutes, or until lightly browned and bubbly.

PRALINE SWEET POTATOES
Makes 10 to 12 servings

6 large sweet potatoes, diced
½ cup butter, softened
1 cup firmly packed light brown sugar
½ cup evaporated milk
½ teaspoon salt
½ teaspoon ground cinnamon
¼ teaspoon ground nutmeg
2 large eggs, lightly beaten
2 cups chopped pecans
¼ cup butter, melted
¼ cup sugar

1. Preheat oven to 350°. In a large Dutch oven, combine sweet potatoes with enough water to cover. Bring to a boil over medium-high heat. Cook for 10 to 12 minutes, or until tender. Drain sweet potatoes well and return to Dutch oven. Add butter; using a potato masher, mash sweet-potato mixture until butter is melted. Add brown sugar, evaporated milk, salt, cinnamon, and nutmeg; whisk to combine well. Whisk in eggs. Spoon sweet-potato mixture into a 13x9-inch baking dish. In a small bowl, combine pecans, melted butter, and sugar, tossing to coat. Sprinkle pecans on top of sweet-potato mixture. Bake for 30 to 40 minutes, or until center is set.

SPINACH AND ARTICHOKE CASSEROLE

Makes about 2½ quarts

2 (10-ounce) packages frozen chopped spinach, thawed and squeezed dry

2 (14-ounce) cans artichoke hearts, drained and chopped

1 (8-ounce) package cream cheese, softened

1 (8-ounce) block fontina cheese, shredded

1 large yellow onion, chopped

1 (8-ounce) can sliced water chestnuts, drained

1 cup sour cream

1 teaspoon garlic powder

¾ teaspoon salt

½ teaspoon ground black pepper

1 (6-ounce) can french-fried onion rings

1. Preheat oven to 350°. In a medium bowl, combine spinach, artichokes, cream cheese, fontina cheese, onion, water chestnuts, sour cream, garlic powder, salt, and pepper. Beat at medium speed with a mixer until well combined. Spoon spinach mixture into a 9x9-inch baking dish. Bake for 35 to 40 minutes, or until bubbly. Sprinkle onion rings on top, and bake 5 minutes more.

STUFFED SQUASH
Makes 10 to 12 servings

6 large yellow squash
½ cup plus 2 tablespoons butter,
  melted and divided
½ teaspoon salt
¼ teaspoon ground black pepper
3½ cups fresh bread crumbs
1 cup sour cream
1 cup finely shredded Cheddar cheese
¼ cup finely chopped green onion
1 tablespoon chopped fresh parsley
1 teaspoon poultry seasoning
¼ teaspoon ground sage
1 large egg, lightly beaten
Shredded Cheddar cheese
Garnish: chopped green onion

1. Preheat oven to 350°. Line a rimmed baking sheet with heavy-duty aluminum foil. Cut squash in half lengthwise. Using a spoon or melon baller, scoop out seeds, leaving shells intact; discard seeds. Place squash on prepared baking sheet. Brush squash with 2 tablespoons melted butter. Sprinkle evenly with salt and pepper.
2. In a medium bowl, combine bread crumbs, remaining ½ cup melted butter, sour cream, cheese, green onion, parsley, poultry seasoning, and sage. Stir in egg. Spoon bread-crumb mixture into squash. Bake for 30 minutes, or until lightly browned. Sprinkle with additional cheese during last 3 minutes of cooking time. Garnish with chopped green onion, if desired.

Decadent DESSERTS

Whether served as a meal's sweet ending or simply as a snowy-day indulgence, these mouthwatering treats are everything dessert should be.

RED VELVET CAKE
Makes 1 (9-inch) cake

1½ cups butter, softened
2 cups sugar
2 large eggs
2½ cups all-purpose flour
½ cup unsweetened cocoa powder
1 teaspoon baking soda
½ teaspoon salt
1½ cups whole buttermilk
1 (1-ounce) bottle red food coloring
1 tablespoon distilled white vinegar
2 teaspoons vanilla extract
Cream Cheese Frosting (recipe follows)
Garnish: chopped pecans

1. Preheat oven to 350°. Spray 3 (9-inch) round cake pans with nonstick baking spray with flour.
2. In a large bowl, beat butter and sugar at medium speed with a mixer until fluffy. Add eggs, one at a time, beating well after each addition.
3. In a medium bowl, combine flour, cocoa powder, baking soda, and salt. Gradually add flour mixture to butter mixture, alternately with buttermilk, beginning and ending with flour mixture. Beat in red food coloring, vinegar, and vanilla. Divide batter evenly among prepared pans. Bake for 25 minutes, or until a wooden pick inserted in center comes out clean. Let cool in pans on wire racks for 10 minutes. Remove from pans, and let cool completely on wire racks.
4. Spread Cream Cheese Frosting between layers and on top and sides of cake. Garnish with pecans, if desired. Store, covered, in refrigerator for up to 2 days.

Cream Cheese Frosting
Makes about 6 cups

2 (8-ounce) packages cream cheese, softened
1 cup butter, softened
1 (1-pound) bag confectioners' sugar
2 teaspoons vanilla extract

1. In a large bowl, combine cream cheese and butter. Beat at medium speed with a mixer until creamy. Gradually beat in confectioners' sugar until smooth. Beat in vanilla.

GERMAN CHOCOLATE POUND CAKE

Makes 1 (10-inch) cake

CAKE:
½ cup butter, softened
2¼ cups sugar
4 ounces German chocolate, melted
5 large eggs
1 teaspoon vanilla extract
2¾ cups all-purpose flour
½ teaspoon baking powder
¼ teaspoon baking soda
¼ teaspoon salt
1¼ cups whole buttermilk
½ cup sweetened flaked coconut
1 cup chopped pecans

CARAMEL ICING:
¼ cup unsalted butter
½ cup dark brown sugar
¼ cup half-and-half
1 cup confectioners' sugar
½ teaspoon vanilla extract
¼ teaspoon salt
Garnish: sweetened
   flaked coconut,
   chopped pecans

1. Preheat oven to 300°. Grease and flour a 10-inch Bundt pan, or spray with baking spray with flour.
2. In a large bowl, combine butter and sugar. Beat at medium-high speed with a mixer until fluffy. Add melted chocolate, beating well. Add eggs, one at a time, beating well after each addition. Add vanilla, beating well.
3. In another large bowl, sift together flour, baking powder, baking soda, and salt. Gradually add flour mixture to butter mixture, alternating with buttermilk, beginning and ending with flour mixture. Stir in coconut and pecans. Pour into prepared pan. Bake for 75 to 90 minutes, or until a toothpick inserted in the center of the cake comes out clean.

Cover cake loosely with aluminum foil during last 20 minutes to prevent excess browning.
4. Let cool in pan for 10 minutes. Remove from pan. Let cool completely on wire rack.
5. In a medium saucepan, melt butter over medium heat. Add brown sugar and half-and-half. Cook, stirring constantly, over medium heat for 2 to 4 minutes, or until smooth. Remove from heat. Transfer to heatproof bowl. Add confectioners' sugar to butter mixture. Beat at low speed with a mixer. Gradually increase speed to medium high; beat until smooth. Add vanilla and salt, beating until smooth. Spoon icing over cooled cake. Garnish with coconut and chopped pecans, if desired.

PUMPKIN BUTTERSCOTCH CRÈME BRÛLÉE
Makes 8 servings

1 (12.25-ounce) jar butterscotch sauce
2 cups whole milk
1 cup heavy whipping cream
2 teaspoons vanilla extract
¼ teaspoon salt
8 egg yolks
1½ cups canned pumpkin puree
3 tablespoons sweetened condensed milk
¾ teaspoon pumpkin pie spice
½ cup sugar

1. Preheat oven to 325°.
2. In a medium saucepan, combine butterscotch sauce, milk, and cream. Cook over medium heat, whisking constantly, for 4 to 7 minutes, or until mixture begins to simmer gently. Add vanilla and salt, whisking well.
3. In a large bowl, whisk egg yolks until well blended. Slowly add 1 cup warm butterscotch mixture, whisking constantly. Slowly add remaining butterscotch mixture, whisking well. Pour three-fourths of the way up 8 ramekins. Place ramekins in a hot-water bath, and bake for 30 minutes, or until center has just set. Let cool to room temperature. Cover tightly, and refrigerate for 3 hours, or until cold.
4. In a medium bowl, combine pumpkin puree, sweetened condensed milk, and pumpkin pie spice, stirring well. Divide evenly among ramekins, smoothing into a layer on top of chilled custard. Sprinkle 1 tablespoon sugar over each custard. Caramelize sugar with kitchen torch or under broiler for 1 to 2 minutes, or until sugar is melted.

CRISP & CREAMY
If you don't have a torch, simply place crème brûlée under the broiler to create a similar melt-away crunch.

CHEESECAKE WITH KUMQUAT AND PINEAPPLE COMPOTE
Makes 1 (9-inch round) cheesecake

CRUST:
2½ cups crushed gingersnaps
6 tablespoons butter, melted
¼ cup sugar
FILLING:
3 (8-ounce) packages cream cheese, softened
1 cup sour cream
1 cup sugar
2 teaspoons vanilla extract
2 large eggs
3 egg yolks
¼ cup heavy whipping cream
¼ cup all-purpose flour
COMPOTE:
2 tablespoons butter
1½ cups halved kumquats
1½ cups diced fresh pineapple
½ cup light brown sugar
¼ cup spiced rum

1. Preheat oven to 300°.
2. In a medium bowl, combine gingersnaps, melted butter, and sugar. Press into bottom and up sides of a 9-inch springform pan.
3. In a large bowl, combine cream cheese and sour cream. Beat until fluffy. Add sugar, beating until smooth. Add vanilla, beating well. Add eggs and egg yolks, one at a time, beating well after each addition. Add cream, beating until smooth. Add flour, beating until smooth. Pour into prepared crust. Place pan on a rimmed baking sheet. Bake for 1 hour to 1 hour and 15 minutes, or until cheesecake is just set in the center. Let cool in oven for 1 hour. Refrigerate for 4 hours or until cold. Remove from pan.
4. In a large saucepan, melt butter over medium heat. Add kumquats, pineapple, brown sugar, and rum. Cook for 15 to 20 minutes, or until kumquats are soft. Let cool at room temperature for 30 minutes. Cover tightly, and chill for 4 hours, or until cold. Spoon over chilled cheesecake.

PEANUT BUTTER CEREAL TREATS WITH CHOCOLATE ICING
Makes about 1½ dozen

10 tablespoons unsalted butter, divided
1 (10.5-ounce) bag mini marshmallows
½ cup plus 2 tablespoons creamy peanut butter
6 cups crispy rice cereal
7 (1.55-ounce) bars milk chocolate, finely chopped
⅓ cup chopped salted peanuts

1. In a large pot, melt 4 tablespoons butter over medium heat. Add marshmallows to butter, and cook for 4 to 5 minutes, or until marshmallows begin to melt, stirring frequently. Add peanut butter, and cook for 3 to 4 minutes, or until marshmallows have melted and mixture is smooth, stirring frequently. Add cereal to marshmallow mixture, stirring to combine.
2. Spray a 13x9-inch pan with nonstick cooking spray.
3. Spoon cereal mixture into prepared pan. Using greased hands, pat into an even layer. Let cool compltely.
4. In a large bowl, combine chocolate and remaining 6 tablespoons butter. Microwave on High in 30-second intervals, stirring between each, until melted and smooth. Spread in an even layer over cereal mixture. Sprinkle with peanuts. Let cool at room temperature until set.

Winter CITRUS AND A TROPICAL *twist* TOP THIS *classic* CHEESECAKE WITH *festive* FLAIR.

CHOCOLATE SILK TART
Makes 1 (9-inch) tart

10 tablespoons unsalted butter,
 melted, divided
2 cups crushed chocolate wafers
¼ cup sugar
2 cups mini marshmallows
1 (14-ounce) can sweetened condensed
 milk
6 ounces unsweetened chocolate,
 chopped
1¾ cups heavy whipping cream, divided
½ cup confectioners' sugar
Garnish: white chocolate curls, milk
 chocolate curls, dark chocolate curls

1. Preheat oven to 350°.
2. In a large bowl, combine 7 tablespoons
melted butter, chocolate wafers, and
sugar. Press into bottom and up sides of a
9-inch tart pan with a removable bottom.
Bake for 10 minutes. Let cool completely.
3. In the top part of a double boiler over
simmering water, combine marshmallows, sweetened condensed milk,
chocolate, and remaining 3 tablespoons
melted butter. Cook over medium heat,
stirring until chocolate and marshmallows
have melted. Add ¼ cup cream, and stir
until smooth. Spoon into prepared pie
crust. Refrigerate for 2 hours.
4. In a large bowl, beat remaining 1½ cups
cream at high speed with a mixer until soft
peaks form. Add confectioners' sugar,
beating until stiff peaks form. Spoon over
chilled pie. Garnish with chocolate curls,
if desired.

PEPPERMINT ROULAGE
Makes 10 to 12 servings

CAKE:
3 tablespoons confectioners' sugar, divided
5 large eggs, separated
¾ cup sugar, divided
½ cup all-purpose flour
1 teaspoon clear vanilla extract
FILLING:
1 cup whipping cream
¼ cup confectioners' sugar
¼ cup finely chopped peppermints
GANACHE:
4 ounces white chocolate, finely chopped
2 tablespoons heavy whipping cream
Garnish: chopped peppermints

1. Preheat oven to 375°. Coat a 15x10x1-inch jelly-roll pan with cooking spray; line with wax paper, and coat wax paper with spray. Dust with 1 tablespoon confectioners' sugar. Set aside.

2. Beat egg yolks at medium speed with a mixer until pale. Add ½ cup sugar, flour, and vanilla, beating well. Set aside.

3. In a medium bowl, beat egg whites at medium-high speed with a mixer until foamy. Add remaining ¼ cup sugar, 1 tablespoon at a time, beating until stiff peaks form. Fold into flour mixture. Spread batter into prepared pan. Bake for 10 to 11 minutes, or until cake springs back when lightly touched in the center.

4. Sift remaining 2 tablespoons confectioners' sugar into a 15x10-inch rectangle on a cloth towel. When cake is done, immediately loosen from sides of pan, and turn onto prepared towel. Peel off wax paper. Starting at narrow end, roll up cake and towel together; place seam side down on a wire rack. Let cake cool completely.

5. In a medium bowl, beat cream at medium-high speed with a mixer until soft peaks form. Add confectioners' sugar, and beat until stiff peaks form. Fold peppermints into mixture.

6. Unroll cake. Spread with peppermint filling. Reroll cake without towel; place seam side down on serving platter.

7. In a small microwave-safe bowl, combine white chocolate and cream. Microwave on Medium for 1 to 1½ minutes or until melted, stirring every 30 seconds. Pour white chocolate ganache over roulage. Garnish with chopped peppermints, if desired.

Family
GATHERING

The joy of the season shines brightly
as families come together to count their blessings
while sharing a traditional Christmas dinner.

THE FINE POINTS

Borrow a few ideas from our friends across the pond to create a British-influenced setting for this family affair. Gather loop-trimmed napkins in polished rings, and pile Christmas baubles in a gravy boat. For a unique, eye-catching display, try this idea: Set pillar candles in glass cylinders filled with a few inches of granulated sugar. Thoroughly dry off fresh cranberries, and layer atop sugar.

ACT NATURALLY

Emphasize winter's beauty with neutral dinnerware and subtle notes of color. Explore decor showcasing the silver side of the season with metallic accents and subdued shades of foliage. Delicate details on platters and glassware add to the elegantly frosted affair.

WHITE CHRISTMAS

Floral arrangements filled with white blooms and a tree trimmed in snowy shades fills the scene with an inviting air. Dress up chairs with cream-colored ribbons, tucking in a bit of varied greenery for good measure.

IN THE DETAILS
Thoughtfully chosen accents lend a festive air to this holiday table. Set out no-fuss hors d'oeuvres to keep guests satisfied until dinner is served. An extravagant floral arrangement and elegant dinnerware nod to the occasion. Patterned tablecloths add a cozy touch, as does the vintage clock—a reminder that time spent with loved ones is the best gift of all.

CHRISTMAS DINNER
Menu

PRIME RIB
Recipe on page 151

ROASTED VEGETABLES
Recipe on page 152

HARICOTS VERTS
Recipe on page 152

RED ONION AND FONTINA TARTS

Makes 1 dozen

1½ (14.1-ounce) boxes refrigerated
    pie crusts
¼ cup butter
2 large red onions, sliced ⅛ inch thick
¼ cup balsamic vinegar
½ teaspoon salt
¼ teaspoon ground black pepper
5 cups shredded fontina cheese
1 (8-ounce) package cream cheese,
    softened
½ cup whole milk
1 large egg
2 tablespoons all-purpose flour
1 tablespoon chopped fresh thyme
½ teaspoon garlic powder
¼ teaspoon seasoned salt

1. Preheat oven to 350°. On a lightly floured surface, unroll pie crusts. Using a 4-inch round cutter, cut 12 circles from crusts. Line 12 (3½-inch) tart pans with crusts; prick bottoms of crusts with a fork. Place on a baking sheet, and bake for 15 minutes; set aside.

2. In a large skillet, melt butter over medium-low heat. Add onions; cover, and cook for 30 minutes, stirring occasionally. Remove cover, and raise heat to medium-high. Add vinegar, salt, and pepper. Cook for 4 to 5 minutes, stirring constantly, until browned; set aside.

3. In a medium bowl, combine cheese and cream cheese. Beat at medium speed with a mixer until creamy. Add milk, egg, flour, thyme, garlic powder, and seasoned salt. Beat until well combined. Evenly divide cheese mixture among crusts. Top with reserved onion. Bake for 20 minutes.

PRIME RIB WITH HORSERADISH CREAM
Makes 8 to 10 servings

2 teaspoons garlic powder
2 teaspoons onion powder
2 teaspoons salt
½ teaspoon ground black pepper
1 (6½- to 7-pound) prime rib
1 tablespoon olive oil
1 recipe Horseradish Cream (recipe
    follows)
Garnish: fresh parsley

1. In a small bowl, combine garlic powder, onion powder, salt, and pepper. Rub prime rib with olive oil and spice mixture. Cover, and refrigerate for 4 hours to overnight. Remove from refrigerator, and let come to room temperature.
2. Preheat oven to 325°. Place prime rib in a roasting pan on a rack. Cook for 2 hours and 45 minutes to 3 hours, or until a meat thermometer inserted into center reaches an internal temperature of 145°, or desired degree of doneness. Remove from oven, and let stand for 10 minutes before carving. Garnish with fresh parsley, if desired. Serve with Horseradish Cream.

Horseradish Cream
Makes about 3 cups

1 (16-ounce) container sour cream
½ cup mayonnaise
3 tablespoons prepared horseradish
2 tablespoons stone-ground mustard
½ teaspoon salt
½ teaspoon ground black pepper
Garnish: fresh chives

1. In a medium bowl, combine sour cream, mayonnaise, horseradish, mustard, salt, and pepper. Cover, and chill for 1 hour before serving. Garnish with fresh chives, if desired.

POPOVERS
Makes 1 dozen

2 cups all-purpose flour
1 teaspoon salt
2 cups whole milk
4 large eggs
¼ cup butter, melted

1. Preheat oven to 375°. Lightly grease a 12-cup popover pan. In a medium bowl, combine flour and salt. In a small bowl, combine milk, eggs, and melted butter, whisking until smooth. Combine milk mixture with flour mixture, whisking until smooth. Spoon batter into prepared pan. Bake for 35 to 40 minutes, or until golden brown. Let cool in pan for 2 minutes. Remove from pan, and serve warm.

PRIMO RIB ROAST

Best served medium rare to well done, this classic special-occasion favorite is bound to cause a stir when the enticing aroma wafts from the kitchen. Though this tender and delicious cut is wonderful on its own, serve it with generous dollops of our horseradish-cream-with-a-kick to truly enhance the flavor.

ROASTED VEGETABLES
Makes 8 to 10 servings

2 pounds carrots, peeled and sliced
  ½ inch thick
2 pounds parsnips, peeled and sliced
  ½ inch thick
2 pounds red potatoes, cubed
4 shallots, sliced
6 tablespoons olive oil
2 tablespoons chopped fresh rosemary
1 tablespoon salt
1½ teaspoons garlic powder
½ teaspoon ground black pepper

1. Preheat oven to 450°. Line a large rimmed baking sheet with aluminum foil; set aside.
2. In a large bowl, combine carrots, parsnips, potatoes, and shallots. In a small bowl, combine olive oil, rosemary, salt, garlic powder, and pepper. Combine vegetables and olive oil mixture, tossing to coat.
3. Bake for 20 to 25 minutes, or until tender, stirring halfway through cooking time.

HARICOTS VERTS WITH PROSCIUTTO AND PINE NUTS
Makes 8 to 10 servings

2 pounds haricots verts
3 tablespoons olive oil
1 (4-ounce) package prosciutto, chopped
½ cup balsamic vinegar
1 tablespoon minced garlic
1 teaspoon salt
¾ teaspoon ground black pepper
½ cup toasted pine nuts

1. In a Dutch oven, place haricots verts and enough boiling salted water to cover; cook for 3 to 4 minutes, or until crisp-tender. Plunge into ice water to stop the cooking process; drain and set aside.
2. In a large skillet, heat olive oil over medium-high heat. Add prosciutto; cook for 3 to 4 minutes, stirring constantly, until crispy. Remove prosciutto from skillet, reserving drippings in pan. To skillet, add vinegar, garlic, salt, pepper, and haricots verts; cook for 3 to 4 minutes, stirring constantly. Top with prosciutto and pine nuts.

SAVORY SQUASH

Children (and finicky grown-ups) will need no prompting to eat their vegetables when they get a taste of this fabulous recipe. Cheese and sour cream take the dish to a whole new level of delight.

BUTTERNUT SQUASH MASH
Makes 8 to 10 servings

3 butternut squash (about 5 pounds)
3 quarts water
1 tablespoon plus 1 teaspoon salt, divided
½ cup butter, softened
1 cup finely grated Parmigiano-Reggiano cheese
½ cup sour cream
1 tablespoon chopped fresh sage
1½ teaspoons fresh lemon juice
½ teaspoon ground red pepper

1. In a Dutch oven, place squash, water, and 1 tablespoon salt. Bring to a boil; cook for 10 to 15 minutes, or until tender. Drain squash well, and return to Dutch oven over medium heat, stirring occasionally, until all water has evaporated. Add butter, stirring until butter is melted. Add cheese, sour cream, sage, remaining 1 teaspoon salt, lemon juice, and red pepper, stirring to combine well.

TASTE OF THE SOUTH

For those who want just a nibble of sweets, a plate of Aunt Aggie De's melt-in-your-mouth pralines is an irresistible option. To order, visit *auntaggiede.com*.

Treat YOUR FAMILY TO A *scrumptious,* SKY-HIGH *chocolate* CAKE.

CHOCOLATE CAKE
Makes 1 (9-inch) cake

3 cups all-purpose flour
2⅔ cups sugar
1 cup unsweetened cocoa powder
2 teaspoons baking soda
1½ teaspoons baking powder
½ teaspoon salt
1⅓ cups whole milk
1⅓ cups butter, melted
4 large eggs
1½ cups sour cream
2 teaspoons vanilla extract
Chocolate Fudge Frosting (recipe follows)
Garnish: chocolate curls, white chocolate curls,
   fresh raspberries

1. Preheat oven to 350°. Spray 3 (9-inch) cake pans with baking spray with flour.
2. In a large bowl, combine flour, sugar, cocoa powder, baking soda, baking powder, and salt. Add milk, melted butter, and eggs; beat with a mixer at medium speed for 2 minutes, or until well combined. Beat in sour cream and vanilla. Spoon batter into prepared cake pans.
3. Bake for 25 minutes, or until a wooden pick inserted in the centers comes out clean. Let cool in pans on wire racks for 10 minutes. Remove from pans, and let cool completely on wire racks. Spread Chocolate Fudge Frosting in between layers and on top and sides of cake. Garnish with chocolate curls, white chocolate curls, and fresh raspberries, if desired.

Chocolate Fudge Frosting
Makes approximately 6 cups

1 cup sugar
1 cup firmly packed dark brown sugar
2 cups heavy whipping cream
8 (1-ounce) squares semisweet chocolate, chopped
1¼ cups cold butter, cut into pieces
2 cups confectioners' sugar, sifted

1. In a medium saucepan, combine sugar, brown sugar, and cream. Bring to a boil over medium-high heat; reduce heat to medium-low, and simmer for 6 minutes, stirring frequently. Remove from heat; add chocolate and butter, stirring until melted and smooth. Let cool for 10 minutes. Gradually whisk in confectioners' sugar. Refrigerate for 1 to 1½ hours, whisking periodically, until chocolate mixture reaches a spreadable consistency.

Acknowledgments

Over the years, we have been blessed by the generosity and hospitality of many homeowners, as well as by our friends at some of the finest stores and companies in the world. To them, we offer our sincerest gratitude for help with the contents of this special volume devoted to celebrating the joys of the Christmas season. If an item is not listed, it is privately owned and not available for purchase. To contact the manufacturers and retail stores referenced, see DIRECTORY OF COMPANIES.

WHITE CHRISTMAS

Page 29: Special thanks to Iris & Co. and Leah Hazzard.

RUSTIC CHARM

Page 42: Special thanks to JR and Lynn Malchus, RKR Construction, Inc., and the Eastern Women's Junior Committee.

CHRISTMAS ON THE MOUNTAIN

Page 48: Special thanks to Wheeler Lewis of Sophie's Shoppe and Stephen DeVries.

SOUTHERN SPLENDOR

Page 56: Special thanks to The Marietta Pilgrimage and Lloyd and Traci Hildreth.

WREATHS FOR THE HOLIDAYS

Page 72: Special thanks to Leah Hazzard and Mandy Majerik.

THE HOLLY AND THE IVY

Page 72: Marco Polo Stemware, Christmas in Your Heart Dinnerware; Rosenthal. Beaded Square Place Mats, Gold Silk Bias Napkins; Kim Seybert. Napkin Rings; Bromberg's. Floral design; Dorothy McDaniel's Flower Market.

O CHRISTMAS TREE

Page 80: Dinner Plate; Vietri. Christmas Tree Plate; Spode.

THE FIRST NOEL

Page 86: Assorted Herend China (Chinese Bouquet, Fish Scale, Golden Edge); Bromberg's.

FAMILY GATHERING

Page 136: Dinner Plates (Johnson Brothers Richmond White); Replacements, Ltd. White Linen Loop Napkins; Kim Seybert.

DIRECTORY OF COMPANIES

ANTHROPOLOGIE, *anthropologie.com*
ARTHUR COURT, *arthurcourt.com*
AT HOME FURNISHINGS, *athome-furnishings.com*
AUNT AGGIE DE'S PRALINES, *auntaggiede.com*
BEVERLY RUFF ANTIQUES, *beverlyruff.com*
BROMBERG'S, *brombergs.com*
CELINE C. RUSSELL, *celinerussell.com*
DOROTHY MCDANIEL'S FLOWER MARKET, *dorothymcdaniel.com*
D.STEVENS, *dstevensllc.com*
EASTERN WOMEN'S JUNIOR COMMITTEE, *ewjc.org*
EXVOTO VINTAGE, *exvotovintage.com*
FOUR SEASONS ANTIQUES, ART & BOTANICALS,
   4seasonsantiquesandart.com
FRENCH LAUNDRY HOME, *frenchlaundryhome.com*
HOBBY LOBBY, *hobbylobby.com*
HOMEWOOD TOY & HOBBY, *homewoodtoy-hobby.com*
HOTHOUSE DESIGN STUDIO, *hothousedesignstudio.com*
INTERNATIONAL SILVER COMPANY, *internationalsilver.com*
IRIS & CO., *irisandcompany.net*
KIM SEYBERT, *kimseybert.com*
JO-ANN FABRIC AND CRAFT STORES, *joann.com*
JOYFOLIE, *joyfolie.com*
JUST PRICELESS, *justpriceless.net*
KAREN ALWEIL STUDIO, *karenalweilstudio.com*
LOWE'S, *lowes.com*
MAISON DE FRANCE, *205-699-6330*
MARIETTA PILGRIMAGE, THE, *mariettapilgrimage.com*
MICHAELS, *michaels.com*
PIER 1, *pier1.com*
PINE HILL FARMS, *pinehillfarms.com*
REPLACEMENTS, LTD., *replacements.com*
RKR CONSTRUCTION, INC., *205-229-3198*
ROSENTHAL, *rosenthalusa-shop.com*
SEIBELS, *205-879-3558*
SPODE, *spode.co.uk*
SWEET PEAS GARDEN SHOP, *sweetpeasgardenshop.com*
TARGET, *target.com*
TREEFORM, *formbyheidi.com*
TRICIA'S TREASURES, *triciastreasures.us*
URBAN SUBURBAN ANTIQUES, *urbansuburbanantiques.com*
VIETRI, *vietri.com*
WENDELL AUGUST, *wendellaugust.com*

"*Peace* ON EARTH WILL COME *to stay*, WHEN WE LIVE *Christmas* EVERY DAY."

—HELEN STEINER RICE